BOEING 747

ALAN J. WRIGHT

LONDON

IAN ALLAN LTD

Previous page:
Unlike many airlines, Kuwait's national flag carrier has not incorporated the country's colours into its livery, preferring the use of an attractive blue on the fuselage and fin. All four 747 combis are painted in this scheme which has the company's title displayed in both English and Arabic. Deliveries began in the summer of 1978, the third becoming 9K-ADC when arrived in the following February. Subsequently the type has maintained the long-haul sectors, although on some timings the 747s are to be found covering stages which are usually the responsibility of the wide-bodied twins.
Peter R. March

First published 1989

ISBN 0 7110 1814 6

Published by Ian Allan Ltd, Shepperton, Surrey; and printed by Butler & Tanner Ltd, Frome and London

INTRODUCTION

Although a commonplace event, the sight of a fully-laden 747 on its take-off run never fails to give the impression that its progress is too leisurely to achieve an airborne state. Having disproved this, its climb away appears equally laborious – the aircraft apparently hanging in the sky, undecided on its future. Of course it is the sheer size of the airliner which provides these illusions for the onlooker; those within notice little difference from any other apart from the spacious cabin proportions. During the past 18 years or so, millions of passengers have flown in the mighty Boeing which certainly revolutionised air travel following its service entry in 1970.

It was as early as 1964 when the USAF initiated a design competition for a large cargo carrier, leading to development contracts being awarded to Boeing, Douglas and Lockheed. Much effort was expended by the three companies, but after extensive studies of the various proposals, Lockheed was given the task of producing the enormous transport which became the C-5A Galaxy. Boeing was naturally disappointed at the outcome, but the research work undertaken at government expense was not wasted. With market research indicating the need for an outsize civil airliner by the 1970s, the company turned its attention to this interesting challenge. Throughout the winter of 1965–66, a number of layouts were considered. Originally a fuselage with a 'double-bubble' cross-section was favoured, but this arrangement did not attract much support from the numerous airlines consulted. Finally, it was a single-deck cabin which was selected with the now familiar 'hump' on top of the forward fuselage containing the flight deck and limited passenger accommodation.

Pan American played a large part in refining the Boeing design, eventually ordering 25 of the monsters on 13 April 1966, although the manufacturer waited until other carriers had committed themselves before giving the go-ahead for production on 25 July. Appropriately, the world's largest airliner required what was to become the world's largest building in terms of volume. A site some 30 miles (48 km) north of Seattle was earmarked for the new structure, which, after only six months, was at a sufficiently advanced stage for 747 work to begin in earnest. Everything associated with the design was large so it was not long before the media began to refer to it as a 'jumbo-sized' airliner. Although somewhat more graceful than an elephant, nonetheless the name was generally adopted until everyone knew of the 'jumbo-jet' even if they had never heard of a Boeing 747.

With such a daunting task, any delay in the completion of the first machine would have been understandable, but as forecast two years earlier the doors of the Everett building opened at 10.30 on 30 September 1968 to allow the 747 to make its debut. Preparations were then made for its maiden flight which of course was eagerly awaited. Originally it had

been expected to take place on 17 December – an appropriate date because it was the anniversary of the Wright brothers' epic flight at Kitty Hawk in 1903. This time the target was not achieved due to tests with the major on-board systems taking longer than anticipated plus the necessary extensive ground-running of the new turbofans. Final checks were made in late January 1969 when high speed taxying trials were satisfactorily completed. Only seven or so weeks behind schedule, the first of the new generation aircraft rolled majestically along the runway for some 4,500 ft (1,370 m) before lifting its 300-ton frame into the air on 9 February. Seventy-six minutes later it was successfully back on the ground for a few minor corrections to be incorporated before its second sortie six days later.

Supporting such an enormous weight called for a robust undercarriage. At an early stage the design utilised 16 main wheels shared equally amongst four bogie units positioned in line abreast, but this formation was changed before production. By moving the under-fuselage pair forward, space was provided for the outer legs to retract sideways and in so doing also ensure that the loads inflicted on airport runways was more evenly distributed. This weight had caused Boeing much trouble as construction proceeded because despite strenuous efforts it steadily increased. To maintain the promised range and payload performance a higher take-off weight was necessary – a requirement which brought new problems in its wake.

Naturally the powerplant had a considerable responsibility in ensuring that the 747 defied gravity, but the engines were also new and suffered their own development setbacks. Each demand for increased thrust brought more difficulties for Pratt & Whitney, but the company managed to develop an uprated specimen of the JT9D although it suffered more than its share of teething troubles before the modified engines settled down to give reliable service with the airlines later in 1970. Meanwhile, flight testing continued apace – the five aircraft dedicated to the task completing the programme and gaining the type's certificate of airworthiness at the end of 1969. During the year one of the batch made the 747's first intercontinental journey when it flew to Le Bourget on the occasion of the Paris Air Show. Visitors were much impressed by the standard of comfort shown in the fully furnished, 382-seat interior.

Back at the factory, 22 aircraft had been rolled-out by mid-October, but alarmingly 17 of these had no powerplant. Subcontractors continued to manufacture components so it was very difficult to slow down assembly without causing still more headaches. Obviously deliveries were likely to be affected – a situation not to the liking of launch customer Pan Am because of the evaporation of any lead advantage over competitors. With two aircraft on strength the airline was able to prepare for the 747's first commercial service – an event which finally took place on 22 January 1970. It was not without incident, however, because earlier a 24-hour delay had been caused by engine trouble. Later, as the aircraft taxied out for its inaugural departure, an overheating JT9D forced a return to the terminal for another six-hour wait. A substitute machine finally made history when it left New York bound for London. The much-heralded age of the jumbo-jet had arrived.

By mid-year many of the major carriers had received their first deliveries. BOAC was one of this group although the airline had a problem of its own to overcome. A dispute between the corporation and it pilots had long been festering with the consequence that after arrival the brand new 747s sat on the ground at Heathrow for almost a year until agreement was reached. As a result of this delay the British flag carrier had not fared well in comparison with other transatlantic operators. Most of those employing the 747 recorded a marked traffic growth, much of which was due to the considerable increase in capacity available. Passenger reaction to the wide-bodied type was mixed, but on the whole they were impressed. Any lack of enthusiasm was usually caused by the poor level of reliability suffered in the early period, but as the improved engines were introduced such criticism was forgotten. As the first operator, Pan Am found several service snags during the first six months. An insufficient number of cabin staff were carried initially and the food trollies were unsatisfactory. It also became apparent that passengers tended to walk around far more than anticipated, thereby hindering the smooth distribution of sustenance. These strollers could also cause embarrassment to others attempting to reach the distant facilities with all speed!

Needless to say, ground handling created plenty of its own problems. New methods were devised at airports so that the greatly increased volume of travellers could be processed

Far left
When sold in 1984, N9669 left American Airlines after some 14 years of service. It did not aspire to follow in the footsteps of its former fleet colleague by seeking employment with NASA – in fact lengthy periods in open storage became a way of life. Owned by the leasing company Citicorp, in 1987 a more active existence was negotiated for the 747 with the Prestwick-based Highland Express. Extensive refurbishment was necessary before the hand-over which introduced unwelcome delays for the new carrier; but finally, resplendent in its freshly applied livery and registered G-HIHO, the aircraft made the transatlantic crossing for the first time. Intended to maintain the company's schedules from Stansted and Birmingham to New York/Newark via Prestwick, the 747 began work towards the end of June 1987. Unfortunately, the late delivery of the aircraft caused some considerable unforeseen expenses for the airline at the worst possible time. Working with only one machine was also not easy on the tight schedules, but nevertheless a route to Toronto was due to be added at the beginning of 1988. Sadly this was not to

(continued overleaf)

(continued)
be, because in mid-December the young carrier went into liquidation after operations spanning less than six months. For G-HIHO it meant the start of another spate of inactivity, this time in Brussels with Sabena, the company entrusted with the 747's maintenance. Attempts to relaunch Highland Express failed, thereby sealing the fate of yet another airline. In due course the 747 left Europe for service with Air Pacific.
Alan J. Wright

Far right
Formed in 1987, Luxembourg-based Lionair's two 747s became a familiar sight in the UK from the beginning of the 1988 summer season after the company began flying transatlantic ITs. Also involved in the contract was the American operator, Orion Air, which explains the presence of this carrier's name on the forward fuselage of LX-GCV. No stranger to Britain, this machine was one of the early batch to see service with Pan Am in 1970 registered N770PA, the identity it retained until transferring to Lionair.
Alan J. Wright

efficiently. It only took a couple of 747 loads to arrive together in order to create chaos. Baggage arrangements had to be reorganised; likewise, caterers had to think in terms of far greater numbers than hitherto. All this happened at a time when there was a general recession looming in the travel industry which quickly removed any prospect of one of the promised benefits expected at the dawn of the wide-bodied era. Instead of the confidently forecast reductions, fares were in fact increased, due in the main to the fuel crisis of 1973. Therefore it was some years before the airlines adjusted themselves to the effects of the 747's arrival, but long before the end of the decade the mighty machine was fully established and accepted by operators and public alike.

A new breed of long-distance traveller was created in the 1970s. European sun-seekers now progressed from the short range IT flights to transatlantic sorties on board the 747s heading for Florida or California. Cheaper fares began to have their effect at last and the capacious cabins were frequently filled. With the introduction of in-flight movies to provide some entertainment during the journey so came the demand for window blinds to be lowered. No longer was it possible to view the snow covered Rockies as the 747 sped along at 35,000 ft without becoming unpopular with the captive audience in the mobile cinema. Maybe it would be better to employ some windowless freighters for those who feel compelled to watch the silver screen.

Boeing had introduced a cargo version early in the type's career, which had first flown on 30 November 1970. Lufthansa became the first carrier to take delivery the following March. An upward-opening nose door provided ease of loading and the design also incorporated a special system for stowing the freight on to the deck. World Airways took delivery of the first convertible 747 in April 1973, only a month or so after its maiden flight. This variant could be used in an all-passenger, all-cargo or combination mode to suit the carrier's needs. As an extension of this theme the mixed load option was assisted by the addition of a large cargo door in the port side of the rear fuselage. This arrangement subsequently became a retrospective modification for airliners previously restricted to carrying passengers. To meet the special requirements of Japan Air Lines, Boeing developed a short range model known as the 747SR. Both structural changes and strengthening were necessary to provide the robustness

for the abnormally high number of landing cycles demanded by the carrier's operations. At the same time, high-density seating was installed to allow 516 travellers to be accommodated.

More obvious changes were visible on the 747SP. Announced in 1973, this model was intended for use on lower-density routes or long range sectors requiring non-stop flights. A reduction in fuselage length of 46 ft 7 in (14.2 m) and an increase in size of the tail surfaces produced a tubby appearance when it entered service with Pan Am in the spring of 1976. Subsequently, several notable record-breaking long distance trips were completed by the airline's machines. Sales were not particularly spectacular and production ceased in July 1982 after 46 aircraft had been built. However, the manufacturer has considered applying the latest technology to the variant in order to create a possible competitor for the Airbus A340 and MD-11.

A more eager reception awaited the series 300 in the mid-1980s. In this case Boeing stretched the familiar upper deck of the standard 747 so that 69 seats could be carried in this compartment. Although produced as a new aircraft, the modified section could also be provided on customers' own machines if required. Internally the method of access to the upper cabin was changed from a spiral to an orthodox straight stairway. Even as this version entered service in 1983 the manufacturer was already developing an updated 747 with an emphasis on efficiency and range rather than increased capacity. When launched as the series 400 it almost immediately out-sold the 300, many operators preferring to bypass the latter to await the latest offering. While retaining the stretched upper deck, the newcomer acquired an increase in wingspan of 12 ft plus the more obvious addition of a 6 ft-tall winglet at each tip. These changes are designed to produce a fuel reduction per passenger mile of 7% compared with the 300's performance. A considerable degree of modernisation has been introduced on to the flight deck which is now designed to be occupied by a crew of two. With typical Boeing showmanship, the 400 was rolled out at Everett on 26 January 1988 while bathed in a wall of laser lights before an estimated 10,000 guests. Slightly later than expected, its first flight took place on 29 April to enable the test programme to begin. After certification the Pratt & Whitney PW4000 powered aircraft was destined for Northwest

Right

It is customary for both cargo and passengers to travel inside the cabin of any airliner, the 747 normally being no exception to this rule. Indeed when N9668 entered service with American Airlines in 1970 it followed these traditions without deviation. Suddenly in 1974 this all changed. At the time the National Aeronautics and Space Administration (NASA) required the services of a transport for its Orbiters without dismantling the substantial airframes for the journey. Chosen for this new role, N9668 was despatched to Boeing for a variety of modifications, the most obvious being the addition of three pylons on the cabin roof and a fin at the tips of the tailplane. Reregistered N905NA, the 747 began its new career in 1977 with a series of test flights from Edwards AFB with the un-manned Orbiter *Enterprise* firmly attached. Then followed three sorties with the astronaut crew on board to give them the opportunity to try out the flight system without actual separation. Finally, on 12 August the Orbiter was released from the mother ship to make its own somewhat faster descent from 24,000 ft for an unpowered landing back at

(continued on next page)

Airlines towards the end of the year. Ten aircraft were ordered by this carrier in October 1985 when it became the launch customer, an example later followed by a further 17 airlines to bring the total number of orders to 118 by the roll-out date. Lufthansa expects to receive the second 400 off the line in March 1989 followed by Cathay Pacific a month later. Power for the latter pair will be provided by General Electric CF6-80C2s and Rolls-Royce RB211-524Gs respectively. Only two months after its maiden trip aloft, the variant was able to claim the world record for the heaviest aircraft take-off. On 27 June it lifted 892,450 lb from Moses Lake Airport, Washington, some 44,100 lb above the normal weight.

So the well-proven giant looks set to take the industry into the next century. No doubt further models will become available as the need arises, with a full length upper deck extension capable of carrying up to 700 passengers a distinct possibility, but at present there is no demand for such capacity. By mid-1988 the total number of orders for the 747 had reached 868 from 72 airlines. Operators of the type at some time or other include:

Aer Lingus, Aerolineas Argentinas, Air Afrique, Air Algerie, Air Canada, Air France, Air Gabon, Air India, Air Jamaica, Air Lanka, Air Madagascar, Air Mauritius, Air National, Air New Zealand, Air Pacific, Air Portugal, Air Siam, Air Zaire, Alia/Royal Jordanian, Alitalia, All Nippon, American Airlines, Avianca, BOAC/British Airways, British Airtours, British Caledonian, CAAC, Cameroon Airlines, Cargolux, Cathay Pacific, China Airlines, Condor, Continental Airlines, CP Air/Canadian Airlines International, Delta Air Lines, Dominicana, Eastern Air Lines, Egyptair, El Al, Evergreen International, Flying Tiger, Garuda Indonesian, Gulf Air, Hawaii Express, Highland Express, Iberia, Icelandair, Iraqi Airways, Iran Air, Iranian Air Force, Japan Air Lines, Japan Asia, Jet 24, KLM, Kenya Airways, Korean Airlines, Kuwait Airways, Lionair, Lufthansa, Malaysian Airline System, Martinair, Metro International, Middle East Airlines, NASA, National Airlines, Nigeria Airways, Northwest Orient, Olympic Airways, Overseas National, Pakistan International, Pan Am, People Express, Philippine Airlines, Qantas, Royal Air Maroc, Sabena, SAS, Saudia, Saudi Royal Flight, Scanair, Seaboard World, Singapore Airlines, South African Airways, Swan Airlines, Swissair, Thai International, Tower Air, Trans International/Transamerica, Trans Mediterranean Airways, Trans World Airlines, United Airlines, United Parcels, USAF, UTA, Varig, Viasa, Virgin Atlantic, Wardair and World Airways. Representatives of some of these are to be found within this book.

base. With tests complete, NASA's unique 747 was thereafter used to ferry the operational Shuttles to the Kennedy launch site in readiness for their exploits, thereby playing an important part in the American space programme.
Peter R. March

Below left
At 10.00 hrs on 7 June 1983, the 747-123 N905NA began its take-off roll along Stansted's Runway 23 to carry the Orbiter *Enterprise* back to the US. As it climbed away there were feelings of relief on the ground that the three-day visit had been so successful. The event certainly caught the imagination of the public who turned out in their hundreds of thousands to choke roads for miles around the Essex airport where a truly carnival atmosphere was created. Many of the anti-airport campaigners used the opportunity to raise funds for repairs to a church roof or two by the sale of home-made rock buns, many of which could have served as material for the renovation. But it was the 747 and its passenger which were deservedly the real attraction to provide a sight few will ever forget.
Alan J. Wright

Right

With 1986 its 60th year of operations, Northwest Orient sponsored the Fighter Meet held at North Weald over the last weekend in June. As the name implies, aircraft of a more warlike nature predominate at this type of function, but an exception was made on this occasion. On both days the airline sent its newly delivered 747-251B N637US to execute some flypasts with a difference. Ambling along at a modest speed, it contrived to formate with Air Atlantique's DC-3 G-AMPY which was suitably adorned in Northwest livery and struggling to match its mighty descendant's progress. During other passes, the 747 was joined by a variety of piston engined fighters, including several Spitfires, a P-47, a Kittyhawk and a Corsair with others valiantly trying to keep up with their unusual formation leader. Dwarfed by the sheer bulk of the airliner, the fighters buzzed around, their pilots thoroughly enjoying this rare opportunity for such an escapade. There is little doubt that the billed appearance of a 747 at a display attracts the crowds in a similar manner to Concorde, the Red Arrows and the Battle of Britain Memorial Flight.

Peter R. March

Left
Northwest's normal activity involves the operation of a vast network of routes throughout the US and Canada, which was considerably increased with the takeover of Republic Airlines in 1986. One of the country's oldest carriers, it was founded in 1926 as Northwest Airlines, but in view of its interests in the East, Orient was added to the title in 1934. Apart from its domestic work, Northwest – as it again became in 1986 – still flies on routes crossing the Pacific, but also includes transatlantic sectors nowadays to link the US with Copenhagen, Dublin, Frankfurt, London, Oslo, Prestwick and Stockholm. Forty passenger and freighter 747s are on strength and the airline became the launch customer for the series 400 in 1985, the first of which should be delivered at the end of 1988. Still with its Northwest Orient titles, N623US is seen landing at Miami, an airport frequently visited by the airline.
Colin Wright

Right

After over eight years with Alitalia as I-DEMB, this 747-243B was returned to Boeing in 1980 for a series of leases lasting until the end of 1984 when the machine was finally purchased by People Express to become N605PE. This carrier was formed in April 1980, its aim being to offer low-cost, high-frequency domestic services in the eastern part of the US; growth came rapidly to take it into transatlantic operations on 26 May 1983. From a single 747 at the outset, the number of the type in service with the carrier steadily grew until eight were on strength in 1986. During the course of the year People Express found itself with increasing financial problems resulting in its sale to the Texas Air Corporation. Consequently, by early 1987 all its activities and fleet had been merged with those of Continental Airlines. Under the new ownership both logo and titles were quickly replaced, but the repainting of the airframe was not attempted at that stage. Accordingly the Continental 747s flew with their People Express livery and registrations throughout the year, but during 1988 they were due to acquire new identities, N33021 being allocated to the depicted specimen.

Robbie Shaw

Right

Edinburgh is seldom visited by 747s, but on this occasion an Alitalia machine (I-DEMG) arrived. Most of the larger UK airports can handle wide-bodied aircraft providing small numbers are involved, but it is not economic to hold numerous sets of the specialist equipment required for each type likely to appear. When weather conditions force diversions, it is therefore necessary to spread the load as evenly as possible between the airports with the means to cope.
British Airports Authority

Bottom left

Northwest has a long history, but the Colombian national airline, Avianca, stretches back even further to the founding of SCADTA in 1919. Based at Bogata, the carrier now undertakes a wide range of domestic services plus links with North and Central America. Long-haul European flights are offered to Frankfurt, Madrid and Paris for which purpose a 747 is employed. This is now registered HK-2980X, but from its delivery in 1979 until 1983 it carried the identity HK-2300 as in the photograph.
Colin Wright

Right

It is a long time since Pan Am's 747-121 N735PA first crossed the Atlantic during a proving flight on 12 January 1970, three days after its delivery to the airline. Since then the machine has been a regular commuter between the US and Europe, although during that time its livery has changed several times – the latest variation ensuring that short-sighted passengers can find it.
Alan J. Wright

Far right

An ex-Braniff machine, the 1970-built 747-127 N601BN is operated by Tower Air both on schedules and charters. Formed in August 1982, the airline took over the routes previously flown by Metro International from New York to Brussels, Oslo, Stockholm and Tel Aviv.
Robbie Shaw

Right

If 747s are not loaded direct from the terminal building then the alternative is usually to employ buses to ferry the travellers to the aircraft. With conditions somewhat akin to the London Underground in a rush hour, this first part of the journey is often undertaken in a standing position until each vehicle in turn arrives at the wide-bodied stairway. If only one door is in use on the aircraft, boarding can take some time, although in wet and windy weather the process speeds up considerably. This picture of a TWA machine shows off the shape of the 747 particularly well.
British Airports Authority

As one of America's leading supplemental carriers, for many years World Airways offered a world-wide range of charters using a variety of aircraft types. In 1973 three 747 combis began work with the company, one of which was N747WA. Although painted in the airline's livery when delivered, the machine spent more time on lease to other carriers than it did with its own operator. In fact for almost five years it stayed with Pan Am as N535PA before returning to World Airways in December 1979. Strangely it never reverted to its full original identity, adopting the suffix WR instead. From this point it was not reregistered although its temporary detachments continued to take it into the hands of National Airlines, Evergreen International, Flying Tigers and Air India. For most of its career it has been used as a freighter, but in a passenger configuration it was equipped with 471 seats. When World Airways drastically reduced its activities in 1986, it restricted its fleet to a few DC-10-30s, so the 747 was never repainted in the new colour scheme chosen by the company.
Boeing

Right

Until the Boeing 747-21AC PH-MCE joined Martinair in the spring of 1987, the airline's long-haul charters were covered by four DC-10-30s. As in the latter case, the newcomer is a combi and when configured for passenger work is equipped with 530 seats. With such a capacity it is also useful for the short European IT sectors in peak periods.
Robbie Shaw

Far right

Air India's VT-EGC is almost at the end of its long journey from Bombay as it crosses the perimeter fence at Heathrow. Last of the airline's 747s to be delivered by Boeing, it arrived some nine years after the first had joined the fleet in 1971. European appearances are not confined to the UK since several other centres on the continent are included in the company's network of routes. India's flag carrier has scheduled links with North America where the gateways are at New York, Montreal and Toronto, while both Perth and Sydney in Australia receive regular visits by the 747s.
Peter R. March

Right
At Amsterdam's Schiphol airport security is often achieved at the perimeter by a series of wide ditches. Fences are therefore unnecessary at these locations which enables uncluttered pictures to be obtained from various vantage points. Since the land alongside the runways is leased to local farmers, aircraft appear to taxy through the middle of a series of small-holdings, the crops varying from cereals to potatoes. Needless to say no livestock is permitted, although the stretches of water provide a home for a multitude of noisy toads. There are several periods in the day when the KLM 747s are particularly active and it therefore does not take long for the fleet to parade before the patient onlooker. In this case the subject is PH-BUC which has been with the airline since May 1971 and is not one of those earmarked to receive the stretched upper deck modification. On the contrary, it will be one of the machines released when the series 406s are delivered in 1989.
Alan J. Wright

Left
Naturally the most common livery to be found on 747s at London is that of British Airways. Some 35 examples made up the fleet in early 1988, but to these will be added the machines inherited by the take-over of British Caledonian. Further additions will occur in the spring of 1989 when the first of the new series 400s arrives, but at this time a start will be made on the retirement of the early fleet members, so the actual numbers on strength will not increase appreciably.
Peter R. March

Right
In November 1970 Sabena took delivery of OO-SGA, the first of a pair of 747-129s. After three years or so both were given a combi layout with a side cargo door for use on the airline's North American and West African services. In October 1986 Sabena began a Brussels-Gatwick- Atlanta service in association with British Caledonian. Originally the agreement was for a one year period, but in fact the services were continued under a temporary permit until the end of March 1988. With the change of partner it is doubtful if the arrangement would have continued anyway.
George W. Pennick

Far right
Jordanian airline Alia was the source of British Caledonian's second Boeing 747 which arrived at Gatwick on 18 March 1985. Still registered JY-AFB, it departed to Paris Orly a few days later for a repaint and a change of identity to G-HUGE. After a lengthy refurbishment the combi eventually entered service on the company's revived Gatwick-New York route on 25 June – a daily commitment which kept the machine fully occupied. After more than two years work for BCal on this and other sectors, it became a victim of the British Airways take-over in late 1987.
Robbie Shaw

Right
Delivered in 1985, D-ABYZ has since been operated by Lufthansa on its long-haul sectors. Like most of its two dozen colleagues in the fleet it is fitted with a side cargo door for mixed working.
Lufthansa

Far right
Becoming a 747 operator in 1973, for the next 10 years or so Olympic Airways found two aircraft sufficient for use on its transatlantic and Far East services. In 1985 the oldest of the pair was sold to TWA, but by this time negotiations had been completed with Singapore Airlines for the purchase of three younger aircraft. Appropriately, the carrier's livery prominently displays the 'six rings' symbol of the Olympic games, but otherwise the colour scheme used is not particularly imaginative.
Boeing

Right

For many years the brightly coloured airliners of CP Air were a familiar sight at the major UK airports from where a large number of Canadian ITs were flown using both DC-10s and Boeing 747s. Of the latter, C-FCRE was one of four acquired in 1973–74 to serve the carrier for over 10 years. A policy of standardisation in 1985 found the quartet leaving the Canadian company for a new career with Pakistan International, 'Romeo Echo' becoming the first to leave in December of that year. Exchanged with an equal number of DC-10s, the newcomers confusingly adopted the same identities as the departing Boeings.
Alan J. Wright

Far right

After a modest entry into the international scheduled scene in March 1945, TAP's network steadily grew until it included transatlantic routes. TAP joined the wide-bodied club in 1972 when it took delivery of CS-TJA, the first of two 747s ordered. Eventually the fleet comprised four of the type, but the second pair did not remain for long before joining Pakistan International. In 1980 the airline was renamed Air Portugal.
Boeing

Wherever El Al's airliners operate there is a considerable
security effort mounted. At some airports a procession is
formed, with armoured vehicles, positioned fore and aft of the
taxying 747 during its journey from and to the active runway,
remaining in attendance during its stay at the terminal.
Fortunately such precautions are not considered necessary
by any other carrier including those of Arab origin. Ironically
the Israeli aircraft often park alongside those belonging to
supposedly hostile nations and indeed it is not uncommon for
cargo to be moved from one machine to another for onward
transportation.
British Airports Authority

Top left
Alia's 747 fleet did not grow a great deal after the first two were delivered in April and May 1977. In fact it was 1981 before another was acquired with all three employed thereafter on the longer transatlantic sectors and some of those within Europe. However, TriStars began to replace the larger type in 1981 resulting in the departure of two 747s to British Caledonian in 1985 and 1987. This left the single specimen (JY-AFA) to ply the New York route for much of its time. In the mid-1980s the airline embarked on a painting spree in an effort to portray a new image. Eventually, after many trial schemes, the chosen livery was predominantly brown and the Royal Jordanian identity was emphasised rather than just that of Alia. In the illustration 'Foxtrot Alpha' is wearing its original 1977 colours.
Boeing

Bottom left
Since taking delivery of the 747 combi CN-RME in 1978, Royal Air Maroc has used it mainly for its transatlantic schedules. These do not over-burden the machine unduly so it also makes regular sorties to the Middle East, an area which creates several high-density routes as a result of ITs designed for pilgrims.
Boeing

Right

Since South African Airways began 747 operations in the early 1970s, the airline has introduced some impressive schedules including non-stop sectors between Johannesberg and European cities. Its 747s roam far and wide but are also to be found on shorter high-density routes. Since ZS-SAN was delivered in October 1971 its livery has been subtly changed although the basic colours remain the same. Nowadays the aircraft carries the letters SAA along the left forward fuselage while on the opposite side the Afrikaanse equivalent SAL appears. On the fin the springbok representation now leaves no room for any other decoration, but the whole design gives the fleet a more modern appearance.
Boeing

Left
Left
To earn its keep a 747 has to spend the majority of its life in the air. Pushbacks across a well-lit airport apron before the start of another night flight were therefore common occurrences for Lufthansa's D-ABYC, one of the airline's first batch of three aircraft delivered in 1970. Its life with the German carrier lasted until January 1979 when it joined Aer Lingus as EI-BED to be configured to carry 468 passengers in an all-tourist layout. During its stay with the Irish airline it has also spent short spells with Air Algerie and Air Jamaica.
Lufthansa

Far left
**As a result of the Falklands
disagreement, Aerolineas
Argentinas no longer serves
London. Nevertheless its
747s are still to be seen
elsewhere in Europe with
flights crossing the south
Atlantic to include Paris,
Frankfurt, Madrid, Rome
and Zurich in the coverage.
For anyone with an
irresistible urge to visit this
South American country it
is therefore necessary to
travel first to one of these
cities. Six 747-200s are on
the strength of the national
carrier, although the after
effects of the 1982 war
necessitated several leases
due to diminishing traffic.**

Left
**Considering the overall
proportions of the 747, the
flightdeck is quite compact.
Looking ahead, the pilots'
view is akin to that from an
attic window while trying to
get the ground floor on to
the runway without it
becoming the basement!
This particular example is
still equipped with electro-
mechanical instruments
but the new 747s have
moved into the age of
cathode ray tube displays
and the associated
electronic control aids. At
the same time the new
cockpit is designed for
operation by two pilots
alone unlike the current
models which all have the
services of a flight engineer.**

Only three 747-200s are employed by the Chinese national carrier, CAAC, B-2450 being delivered in the spring of 1987. To the right of its fin can be seen the tail of N1304E (now B-2452), one of four SP variants also flown by the airline. With this somewhat plain livery the most outstanding feature is the large national flag carried on the fin. Scribed in Chinese along the fuselage sides is the airline's title, but, for the benefit of those unable to read the language, CAAC is repeated in small characters in the vicinity of the flight deck. Those adept with a paint brush will have plenty of practice when the airline takes up the identity of Air China.
Robbie Shaw

Left
Formed in 1946, Cathay Pacific employed DC-3s in those early days, launching scheduled services two years later. Now recognised as the Hong Kong flag carrier despite being privately owned, the company serves centres in the Middle and Far East, Australia, Europe and North America. Only wide-bodied aircraft are now used, the first of the 747s joining the fleet in 1980. Eight passenger carrying series 200s are now on strength, of which VR-HIE was the fifth to arrive. Another pair perform their duties as freighters while the latest additions have been the stretched upper deck variant, the type which maintains the longer range sectors. Although the runway has water alongside it, the mountain in the background confirms that the 747 is not landing at London City!
Robbie Shaw

Right

Clustered around Tokyo's Narita terminal are four of the 60 or so 747s of all models operated by Japan Air Lines. In the foreground is JA8115, one of five standard series 100s in service while at the rear of the group a stretched upper deck series 300 can be seen. Red and black are the only colours used in the company's livery which, on the upper surfaces of the wings, includes the familiar red disc generally associated with the country. JAL operates over a large network of international routes, but lost its monopoly in 1986 when All Nippon introduced services to Guam. However, as compensation the Japanese national carrier was able to launch its first new domestic sectors since 1972. From April 1986, non-stop flights have been offered between Tokyo and both London and Paris.
Robbie Shaw

After some years Philippine Airlines has adopted a more modern livery for its fleet which includes four Boeing 747s – all of which entered service in 1980. Based on the national flag, the fin marking differs from that previously carried by the addition of a sun-burst design appearing from behind the red segment. It was intended to signify a new beginning for the country at the end of a 14-year-long dictatorship. In a similar manner to its three colleagues, N742PR has continued to be identified by a US registration rather than by one allocated in the Philippine's series. Their duties take them on long-haul international sectors to the Middle East and Europe where regular visits are made to Amsterdam, Athens, Frankfurt, London/ Gatwick, Paris, Rome and Zurich. Schedules are also flown to the west coast of the US at Los Angeles and the Pacific island of Hawaii.
Robbie Shaw

Top right

Externally there is little to distinguish JA8152 from any other standard 747 in the 100 series. However, the 747SR was developed as a short range, high-density version aimed particularly at the Japanese market. All Nippon operates domestic and regional services with the type which it first took on strength at the end of 1978. Since then a total of 17 have joined the fleet which has steadily shed the pale blue livery worn for some years by such as JA8152.
Robbie Shaw

Bottom right

All Nippon's latest colour scheme is well illustrated by JA8133, which was in fact the first 747SR-81 to join the airline in December 1978. Formed in 1958 from the merger of Far Eastern Airlines and Japan Helicopter & Aeroplane Transport Co, All Nippon has since become the country's largest airline, although it was March 1986 before its first international scheduled service was launched to link Tokyo with Guam. Routes to both Los Angeles and Washington followed in July and in due course the carrier hopes to serve European cities. Already six 747-200s are on strength for this type of operation and on order are 11 of the new series 400.
Robbie Shaw

As could be expected, Nippon Cargo Airlines (NCA) is
associated with All Nippon, but in this case its fleet contains
three 747 freighters with a fourth machine on order. Delivered
in February 1985, JA8168 was the second aircraft to arrive
before scheduled cargo services were started on 8 May. The
company was actually formed in September 1978, the
lengthy delay in beginning operations being due to a civil
aviation policy review conducted by the Japanese authorities.
New York and San Francisco are now visited by NCA's aircraft
six times each week, while Hong Kong is the destination on
two occasions in the same period, all services radiating from
Tokyo.
Robbie Shaw

Right

In addition to a wide range of domestic and international passenger schedules, Korean Air also uses its four 747 freighters for regular flights to airports in Europe, the US and the Far East. Seen touching down at Hong Kong is HL7452, which has also spent some time on lease to Saudia since its delivery in 1980.
Robbie Shaw

Far right

The company which formed as Seaboard and Western in 1947 later adopted the title Seaboard World before going on to become one of America's leading cargo carriers by providing regular international services. It soon found itself operating on behalf of other airlines such as Viasa and Saudia, carrying the additional titles on the fuselage alongside those of its owner. However, from 1977 Flying Tiger Line steadily acquired an interest in the company until finally, on 1 October 1980, Seaboard World was completely taken over and merged into its rival. Quick to disappear was the smart gold and white livery, while new identities were allocated to the fleet, N701SW becoming N811FT with its new owner.

Right

Simple but effective is the livery of Flying Tigers, the first all-cargo airline in the US. Formed in 1945, the present title was adopted a year later. For many years the carrier confined most of its work to the American continent and trans-Pacific scheduled freight services. In order to expand its interests across the Atlantic to Europe, the company acquired Seaboard World in October 1980, thereby gaining access to this new market for its large fleet which was further increased in size by the newcomers. One of the 747s affected was N704SW which nowadays flies in FTL's livery with the identity N814FT.
Robbie Shaw

Now France's largest independent airline, UTA was created in 1963 by the amalgamation of UAT and TAI, a pair of carriers dedicated to maintaining links with the former French Territories in West Africa. These destinations still account for much of UTA's work with 25 different points visited both on passenger and cargo services. However, its activities are not confined to this area since its network also embraces the Far East, Australia, New Zealand, some of the Pacific islands and the west coast of the US. A large volume of freight is handled by the company which employs the 747 F-GBOX exclusively for this work backed up by four combi machines – two each of the 200 and 300 series.
Robbie Shaw

When granted independence, the former French colonies in
Africa found it impossible to own an airline individually for
financial reasons. Nevertheless, to ensure survival it was
essential that air transport was readily available, so as a
solution 11 states pooled resources in March 1961 to create
Air Afrique as their official carrier. Services have since been
maintained on regional routes throughout Africa as well as
providing regular links with France where strong ties still
exist. Air Afrique began its association with the 747 in October
1980 when it received the freighter TU-TAP for use on its
cargo services. Gainful employment was found until March
1984 when a series of leases saw the end of the machine's
service with the airline. However, it is anticipated that a combi
version will be joining the fleet to renew the carrier's
acquaintance with the type.
Boeing

Left

This specialised freighter version of the 747 was developed early in the type's career, flying for the first time on 20 November 1971. Certificated during the following March, it was almost immediately delivered to Lufthansa the German national carrier becoming the first to operate the variant. An increasing number of airlines are taking up the option to have a side cargo door installed to speed up further the loading and unloading process. A regular visitor at major airports around the world, special lifting devices are used to raise the freight pallets to the 747's floor level at which point the aircraft's own system can be employed to handle and stow the load.

Far left
Few personnel are necessary during the loading of a 747 freighter providing the lifting devices are available. Air France, which is one of the larger carriers undertaking freight work in addition to its extensive passenger operations, employs seven specialist aircraft, each of which also has the side door fitted. Stansted has a growing involvement in cargo handling and it is at the Essex airport that F-BPVR was seen ingesting its latest consignments.
British Airports Authority

Left
Rolls-Royces are loaded onboard Japan Air Lines 747-246F (SCD) JA8171.
BAA/Arthur Kemsley

Right
Stansted by night: Flying Tiger Line 747-249F(SCD) N810FT *Clifford G. Groh* **prepares to receive a consignment of cargo. At present the apron provided for such activities can only accommodate one 747 so a speedy turn-round is essential.**
BAA/Arthur Kemsley

Far right
Showing off its distinctive squat appearance is the first of Braniff's 747SPs. One of the older and larger US airlines, Braniff ordered three with deliveries to begin in 1979 – October of that year marking the arrival of N603BN. Orange was a popular colour with the company although it was by no means standard for all the fleet. Used for a short time on the carrier's long range non-stop sectors, the SPs were not destined to remain long in Braniff's employ. After barely a year N603BN retired for a period of storage with Boeing which finally ended in 1985 when it took up a new life in Oman. In the meantime its former owner had gone into liquidation and the fleet had dispersed anyway.
Boeing

Far left
During the early 1980s Air Mauritius employed Boeing 707s on its international sectors, but the need to offer more modern equipment found the carrier leasing a 747SP from South African Airways with another from the same source joining the airline in 1987 to become 3B-NAJ. The type is used on European routes which includes those serving London, Paris, Rome and Zurich.
George W. Pennick

Left
In some States wars tend to interrupt normal activities, but Iran's national carrier has managed to operate its 747SP-86s without a great deal of attention from the opposition. Iran Air became the second airline to take delivery of the variant in March 1976, that illustrated (EP-IAB) following two months later. Surprisingly there are travellers in sufficient numbers to justify three visits per week to the UK.
British Airports Authority

Far left
One of the current users of the 747SP, Syrianair was an early customer for the variant, taking delivery of YK-AHA in May 1976. This was followed two months later by the second and last. Subsequently, the pair have been used on the airline's longer routes, although these are relatively few and do not extend across the Atlantic. Although the national flag is reproduced on the side of the rear cabin, the carrier's livery does not include any red or black, but instead uses blue for the cheat line and fin.
British Airports Authority

Left
For many years the Australian flag carrier has operated an all-Boeing fleet made up of 747 variants and the 767. Included in the former are a pair of 747SPs which were acquired by the airline in 1981 for use on the long trans-Pacific services to the west coast of America. First to arrive was VH-EAA wearing the livery of the period, but since delivery the airline has adopted a more modern all-white scheme with a red fin and rear fuselage.
Boeing

Unlike its neighbour, CAAC, China Airlines is less reluctant to display its title in English using letters as large as those employed for the national language. As the national carrier for the Republic of China based in Taiwan, a number of 747s are operated on international scheduled services which include routes to New York, Los Angeles and Amsterdam, the latter being the only European city currently visited. Amongst the fleet are four of the SP version, N4508H being one of them. Originally this was destined to become B-1882, but because the machine was leased it adopted a US identity instead, a practice which is not uncommon nowadays.
Robbie Shaw

Left
The 747 approaching in this view is N141UA, an SP belonging to United Airlines. Back in 1975 it was the second of the type to fly and was part of the batch ordered by Pan Am. For some months it remained with the manufacturer, but with tests complete it joined its intended owner in May 1976 as N531PA. Thirteen SPs eventually joined the airline and were used on a number of long haul routes until circumstances forced Pan Am to sell some of its assets. These included all the Pacific operations and some 18 aircraft, the majority of which were the 747SPs. Therefore, in February 1986 United formally took over the machines, in due course reregistering them in its own sequence.
Robbie Shaw

Left

Swissair was a launch customer for the stretched upper deck variant of the 747, taking delivery of its first (HB-IGD) in March 1983. Equipped with a side cargo door, this combi version is configured with 261 seats in three classes while its freight load varies with the routes upon which it is employed. Together with the three others operated by the national carrier, HB-IGD is normally employed on the long range services between Zurich and North America or the Far East. When delivered the series 300s displaced two 747s which had been with the airline since early 1971.
Robbie Shaw

Above

Appropriately, the stretched upper deck 747-300s belonging to Singapore Airlines have all had the inscription 'Big Top' painted to the rear of the flight deck. In most cases the aircraft carry a US registration which incorporates the last two letters of the mark allocated by the Singapore authorities but which remained unused. For example the specimen depicted is identified as N123KJ rather than 9V-SKJ as originally intended. It is one of 14 in service with SIA which maintains a policy of operating a young fleet. Routes to some 50 destinations are now served by the carrier which did not begin operations until October 1972.
Robbie Shaw

Japan Air Lines also favours the use of the 747SR high-density version for its domestic services, but unlike All Nippon the airline has some series 300s in its fleet. Used for the long international sectors, JAL was an early customer for the variant, taking delivery of N212JL in 1983. Later the extended cabin also proved an attractive idea for increasing still further the capacity of the 747SR. Two were therefore ordered for delivery in 1988, each aircraft having the ability to carry 563 passengers. Upon arrival the newcomers were expected to release some of the older specimens for relatively early retirement – an event brought about by the high number of landings made by machines used on short sector working.

Peter R. March

Amongst the assorted types operated by Saudia are 10 747-300s, HZ-AIT being the last of the batch when delivered in 1986. As the largest Middle East carrier, the airline operates scheduled passenger and cargo services to points in the Far East, Africa, Europe and the US. The daily sorties between Jeddah and London are all covered by the large capacity 747s, such is the traffic generated. Whatever the practical benefits derived from the extended upper cabin, the classic lines of the original 747 design are difficult to improve.
Robbie Shaw

Far left
All three of Sabena's 747s are combi versions although OO-SGC is the only series 300 in the fleet, joining the original pair in June 1986. With Belgium still having links with its one-time African colonies, the routes to the continent can use the greater capacity of the type, but it is also to be found on many of the long-haul sectors as required. It seems unlikely that Sabena will increase its 747 fleet, concentrating instead on its new long range A310s.
Boeing

Left
Although Boeing did not win the contest to supply the USAF with an outsized transport, it subsequently received an order for four 747s to be used for special duties by the military. Known as the E-4A/B, all are employed by No 1 Airborne Command and Control Squadron and are operated only in the US unlike the earlier E-3 version of the 707. In times of war the flying command centres would be able to direct the nation's efforts from above the conflict, hopefully to bring a successful conclusion before running out of fuel. This particular example was the last of the batch and received the identity 50125.
Boeing

Right

Two for the price of one – a shot achieved by zooming the lens rather than moving the 747. After 1992 it may serve to bring back fond memories of the days when duty-frees made such views possible even without a camera!

Far right

British Airways is unlikely to change its livery before the first of the new 747-436s arrives in 1989. However, this artist's impression also serves to illustrate the two main external differences between the newcomer and the earlier variants. Following the popular fashion, the aircraft has grown a winglet at each tip and also incorporates the extended upper deck introduced on the preceeding series 300. Registrations in the range commencing G-BNLA have been reserved for the newcomers.
Boeing

The end.
Lufthansa